Healing From Trauma: A Christian Perspective

MELISSA TAYLOR, MSW

DEDICATION

This book is first and foremost dedicated to Joey, my everything; to Russell, the arrow in my quiver; to Jed, who saw me at my worst and beat the roof down so I could be lowered to Jesus; and to mom, whom I love no matter what.

CONTENTS

INTRODUCTION

Because trauma so often stems from ruptured social connections, healing from trauma best occurs within a restorative social setting. We all need each other in the body of Christ, especially during moments of spiritual reflection and growth. Therefore, this book is meant to be a companion piece that accompanies your healing journey while you walk with Jesus and your fellow believers.

Many elements of this book require personal journaling and sharing your experience with a trusted friend. You will need at least one Christian brother or sister who can regularly pray with you and encourage you as you explore your pain and grief.

This book is written from the Christian perspective and seeks to ease suffering through the power of Jesus Christ and the words in the Bible. As you go through this process, you also may need to seek the counsel of behavioral health specialists or psychiatrists if your mental health symptoms become unmanageable.

Before we begin, it will be helpful to understand the "Assumptions of Healing[1]" that are adhered to throughout this process. You may find it helpful to review these core beliefs from time to time as you read this book.

ASSUMPTIONS OF HEALING
1. God's Word is alive and active. It can cut through what is going on in our minds and bodies (Hebrews 4:12). God's Word speaks to us through the Holy Spirit (John 14:26).
2. God is good and full of love. The enemy comes to steal, kill, and destroy. God is not the cause of suffering; He is the cure to suffering. Sin in the world is the cause of suffering (James 1:12-18).
3. God created emotions to help us and protect us. They are not right or wrong. Instead, they are clues that help us know what is going on in our minds and bodies.
4. The reason why we seek healing is to become more fully functioning members of the body of Christ (2 Corinthians 1:3-4).
5. Healing comes from focusing on what God leads us to change in our own lives, not by focusing on the things that we want others to change.
6. We do not qualify or question our experience of suffering. Pain is pain regardless of how "much" or how "little" we were harmed. No one's pain is greater or less than the other.

CHAPTER 1: IDENTITY

The foundation of healing rests in our identity. Before we can further explore our emotions, thoughts, or behaviors, we must discover the Biblical answers to the questions *"Who is God"* and therefore, *"Who am I?"* Our answers to these core questions will greatly shape our healing experience.

God has chosen to reveal Himself to His creation through the Bible. The God of the Bible eternally exists as three distinct Persons– the Father, Son, and Holy Spirit.[2] In *The God of the Bible, an Introduction to the Doctrine of God*, Robert Lightner provides this definition about God's nature:

"God is Spirit. He is a living and active divine Person who is infinite, eternal, and unchangeable in His being, wisdom, power, holiness, justice, goodness, truth and love. He can enjoy fellowship with persons He created in His own image and redeemed by His grace, and He always acts in harmony with His perfect nature.[3]"

Let's explore what the Bible says about the three distinct Persons of God.

God the Father

Ephesians 4:6 (NLT) describes God the Father by saying, "one God and Father of all, who is over all, in all, and living through all."

God the Son

Colossians 1:15–19 (NLT) describes God the Son by saying, "Christ is the visible image of the invisible God. He existed before anything was created and is supreme over all creation, for through Him God created everything in the heavenly realms and on earth. He made the things we can see and the things we can't see– such as thrones, kingdoms, rulers, and authorities in the unseen world. Everything was created through Him and for Him. He existed before anything else, and He holds all creation together. Christ is also the head of the church, which is His body. He is the beginning, supreme over all who rise from the dead. So He is first in everything. For God in all His fullness was pleased to live in Christ."

God the Holy Spirit

1 Corinthians 2:10 (NLT) describes God the Holy Spirit by saying, "But it was to us that God revealed these things by His Spirit. For His Spirit searches out everything and shows us God's deep secrets."

Who Am I?

The Bible describes humans as having a spirit, soul, and body. In 1 Thessalonians 5:23 (NLT), Paul writes, "Now may the God of peace make you holy in every way, and may your whole <u>spirit</u> and <u>soul</u> and <u>body</u> be kept blameless until our Lord Jesus Christ comes again." Another way of describing our human experience is to say, "I have a spirit that has a soul that is housed in a body that lives in the natural world[4]." Let's examine each part in more detail.

Spirit

Our spirit was created by God so that we can contact and receive Him. Therefore, we must use our spirit to connect with God. John 4:24 (NLT) says, "For God is Spirit, so those who worship Him must worship in Spirit and in truth." The way a radio functions is a good illustration of our spirit's unique ability to contact and receive God[5]. When a radio is turned on and properly tuned, it can receive the invisible radio waves in the air and interpret them[6].

Soul

Our soul is comprised of our mind, will, and emotions. It is your personal thumbprint; what makes you different from everyone else[7].

Body

Our body is made up of muscles, organs, and bones. We perceive the five senses of touch, sight, smell, taste, and hearing using our body.

The Human Dilemma

God's glorious standard is for our spirit to be connected to His Spirit so that we can hear His truth. Our soul should have Him at the center of our will, mind, and emotions. Our bodies should glorify Him in everything we do. We all know this is not the case. Romans 3:23 (NLT) says, "For everyone has sinned; we all fall short of God's glorious standard." We cannot be healed from our trauma until we face the greatest trauma of all: our separation from God.

How can God's Holy Spirit live in us when we are sinful and corrupted? Our spirit has turned to other things and we are not tuned into His voice. Romans 8:7-8 (NLT) says, "For the sinful nature is always hostile to God. It never did obey God's laws, and it never will. That's why those who are still under the control of their sinful nature can never please God."

Our minds and bodies have been led astray and are now heading towards death. Paul wrote, "So letting your sinful nature control your mind leads to death" (Romans 8:6, NLT) and "the wages of sin are death" (Romans 3:23, NLT).

God's Gift of Salvation

Healing will start in our souls and bodies after our spirits are tuned into God's Spirit. We can only experience true transformation if we can be reborn and remade into a person who is connected to God again. How can this be done? God has done the impossible by rescuing us from death and making us a new creation. He has provided a way to make us without sin and to be a temple that can house His Spirit in our bodies. Here is what the Bible says about God's solution to this dilemma:

"…through Jesus, God has reconciled everything to Himself. He made peace with everything in heaven and on earth by means of Christ's blood on the cross. This includes you who were once far away from God. You were His enemies, separated from Him by your evil thoughts and actions. Yet now He has reconciled you to Himself through the death of Christ in His physical body. As a result, He has brought you into His own presence, and you are holy and blameless as you stand before Him without a single fault." Colossians 1:20-22, NLT

"Each of you must repent of your sins and turn to God, and be baptized in the name of Jesus Christ for the forgiveness of your sins. Then you will receive the Holy Spirit." Acts 2:38, NLT

"This means that anyone who belongs to Christ has become a new person. The old life is gone; a new life has begun!" 2 Corinthians 5:17, NLT

"Don't you realize that all of you together are the temple of God and the Spirit of God lives in you?" 1 Corinthians 3:16, NLT

"So now there is no condemnation for those who belong to Christ Jesus. And because you belong to Him, the power of the life-giving Spirit has freed you from the power of sin that leads to death." Romans 8:1-2, NLT

"But you are not controlled by your sinful nature. You are controlled by the Spirit if you have the Spirit of God living in you." Romans 8:9, NLT

"My old self has been crucified with Christ. It is no longer I who live, but Christ lives in me. So I live in this earthly body by trusting in the Son of God, who loved me and gave Himself for me." Galations 2:20, NLT

"God saved you by His grace when you believed. And you can't take credit for this; it is a gift from God. Salvation is not a reward for the good things we have done, so none of us can boast about it. For we are God's masterpiece. He has created us anew in Christ Jesus, so we can do the good things He planned for us long ago." Galations 2:8-10, NLT

End of Chapter Reflection

Take a moment to journal through the following questions:

1) What does it mean for my identity to be immersed in the core questions of "Who is God" and "Who am I?"
2) Do I embrace the definition of the human dilemma and God's solution to fix it?
3) Do I trust God enough to begin this healing journey with Him?

CHAPTER 2: TRUST

After you have become a new creation, God's Spirit dwells in you. True healing begins to take place as His Spirit restores our souls and bodies. We will be using Psalm 23 as a road map for healing. Psalm 23:1 says, "The Lord is my shepherd; I shall not want" (ESV). What does this mean? This verse suggests that God is our guide on the path to healing. He is our only source for joy and peace. We must follow Him and accept that He holds the answers for our lives.

The Bible includes many stories of how God healed His people. His healing process follows a pattern, which we can remember with the acronym CPR. He first (C)ALLS us, then (P)ROTECTS us, then (R)EPAIRS us. Let's examine each step of healing in more detail.

Calls Us

Before God delivers His law to His people and requires them to change, He always saves them first. He calls them to Himself and gives them His salvation before telling them to obey. For example, many of us have heard the ten commandments from Exodus 20, but it should be noted that God gave these commandments after He demonstrated His glorious power by saving His people from slavery in Exodus 14. This is what He does for all of

His children. He rescues us so that we can trust His power.

Protects Us

Next, God surrounds His people with love. This love is continuous and all-encompassing. Once you become God's child, He lovingly pursues you with the undying love of a faithful parent. After saving His people from slavery in Exodus, He says this before giving them the ten commandments: "You have seen what I did to the Egyptians. You know how I carried you on eagles' wings and brought you to Myself. Now if you will obey Me and keep My covenant, you will be My own special treasure from among all the peoples on earth; for all the earth belongs to Me" Exodus 19:4-5, NLT.

We can build trust in God by imagining the comfort of riding on the wings of an eagle, safe from evil. Psalm 91:4 (NLT) says, "He will cover you with His feathers. He will shelter you with His wings. His faithful promises are your armor and protection." God knows that we can't hear His law and make changes until we are covered in His feathers, surrounded by His love.

Isaiah 61:10 gives us an imagery of God's salvation by comparing it to a robe and jewelry. "I am overwhelmed with joy in the Lord my God! For He has dressed me with the clothing of salvation and draped me in a robe of righteousness. I am like a bridegroom dressed for his wedding or a bride with her jewels" (NLT).

Before we step out in faith and follow our Shepherd down new paths of change, we must have confidence in our standing with Him. We have to feel the weight of the robe of righteousness on our shoulders. We have to envision the jewels He has covered us with because we are now gorgeously perfect in His sight. We have to believe that this robe cannot be removed because God has placed it on us. We are loved forever and nothing can change that.

Repairs Us

After God has called us and protected us with His love, He begins to change us. He never asks us to change by our own strength. Instead, He asks us to stay weak and admit our need for Him. This weakness and inability to change gives God a chance to use HIS power to change us. Our lives become a testimony that preaches the power of God to transform us. 2 Corinthians 3:16-18 says, "But whenever someone turns to the Lord, the veil is taken away. For the Lord is the Spirit, and wherever the Spirit of the Lord is, there is freedom. So all of us who have had that veil removed can see and reflect the glory of the Lord. And the Lord– who is the Spirit– makes us more and more like Him as we are changed into His glorious image" (NLT).

End of Chapter Reflection

Take a moment to journal through the following questions:

1) Am I ready to follow the Shepherd down a path of healing?
2) Do I believe Jesus has the ability to heal me?
3) Do I believe that Jesus is willing to heal me?
4) Am I confident in my standing with God?

CHAPTER 3: REST

The next stop on our healing journey is to tackle the problem of suffering. Where does it come from? Psalm 23:2 paints a picture of a gentle Shepherd leading His child to a beautiful pasture with soft green grass and a bubbling brook. The verse says, "He makes me lie down in green pastures. He leads me beside still waters. He restores my soul" (ESV).

But what if life has been the opposite of this? Where was God then? It is important to remember that sin is the cause of suffering. James 1:13 says, "God is never tempted to do wrong, and He never tempts anyone else" (NLT). Ezekiel 18:32 says, "For I have no pleasure in the death of anyone, declares the Lord God; so turn, and live" (ESV). God also says, "If anyone does attack you, it will not be My doing; whoever attacks you will surrender to you" (NIV).

The Beginning and End of the Human Experience
We know that sin is the cause of suffering because the Bible shows us the beauty of God's created world before sin entered the picture. The chart on the following page outlines the characteristics of this safe haven that God created for humanity.

Plants, fruit trees, oceans and sea creatures, sky with birds, animals	Genesis 1:11, 20, 21, 25
Humans' job is to care for the garden and the animals	Genesis 1:26; 2:15
Man and woman are in a harmonious relationship with one another	Genesis 2:24-25
God openly speaks with humans and directs their lives	Genesis 2:16, 3:8-9

After sin enters God's created world, we see that the safe haven is disrupted. The land is no longer sprouting plants and fruit trees. Humans can no longer care for the garden and the animals. Man and woman are now against each other, blaming each other and walking in shame. Their children murder each other. They are not in open communication with God at all times.

Suffering enters the scene at the beginning of creation and through Jesus' suffering, it will end when He returns. 1 Corinthians 15:21-22 (NLT) says, "So you see, just as death came into the world through a man, now the resurrection from the dead has begun through another man. Just as everyone dies because we all belong to Adam, everyone who belongs to Christ will be given new life." Isaiah 53:4-5 says, "Yet it was our weaknesses He carried; it was our sorrows that weighed Him down. And we thought His troubles were a punishment from God, a punishment for His own sins! But He was pierced for our rebellion, crushed for our sins. He was beaten so we could be whole. He was whipped so we could be healed" (NLT).

We know that suffering will end because of Jesus' death and resurrection because the Bible shows us how God will restore this earth when He returns. This chart outlines the characteristics of this restored world that God will create for humanity, according to Revelation chapters 21 and 22.

Tree of life on each side of a river. The leaves are medicine to heal the nations	Revelation 22:2
God will live among His people in constant communion with them	Revelation 21:3
God wipes every tear from our eyes; no more death or sorrow or crying or pain	Revelation 21:4

While living between the perfect garden in Genesis and the restoration of the earth in Revelation, it's easy to notice all the dead grass and murky water all around us. How can Jesus lead us to green pastures and still water? It starts by understanding the root of suffering and understanding that God is the answer. Trauma is not of God and He is good. Trauma is relational and it occurs when we sin against each other.

The chart below provides a snapshot of how we create meaning from events that have happened to us. Our beliefs about suffering can become distorted through the lens of our experiences.

Event	Belief	Emotion	Behavior	Consequences
Any event or circumstance that impacts us; Events that affected how we adapted and protected ourselves (may or may not have a specific memory of it)	How we interpret events. Always come before an emotion. Formed from our environments growing up. How did we learn about emotions from family, culture, etc?	What we feel

4 Core Emotions: Anger, Fear, Sadness, Happiness | What we do | The external events that occur as a result of our behavior |

Chart is adapted from Albert Ellis' ABC Model & Brenda Cochran's Whole Person Framework Theory

Let's review the chart on the following page to explore how distressing events in our lives can lead to different beliefs about the cause of suffering. The first two beliefs about suffering are false, which lead to anguish and destructive consequences. The third belief is according to the Bible, which leads to peace and positive outcomes.

Event	Belief	Emotion	Behavior	Consequences
Any event or circumstance that impacts us;	*How we interpret events.*	*What we feel*	*What we do*	*The external events that occur as a result of our behavior*
Rejected or Abandoned by a loved one	[False belief] God caused this suffering	Rejected and abandoned by God and people; despair; alone	Self-harm, substance use, reckless actions	Poor health, injury, possible encounters with criminal justice system
Rejected or Abandoned by a loved one	[False belief] I am the cause of this suffering; it's my fault	Self-hatred; doubt that God cares; a desire to distance from others	Self-harm, substance use, reckless actions	Poor health, injury, possible encounters with criminal justice system
Rejected or Abandoned by a loved one	[True, Biblical Belief] Sin is the cause of this suffering. The other person chose to sin and I am suffering from the fall out of their sin.	A desire to cling to God for relief; hope; compassion for self and others; open to reconciliation; peace inside	Seek God's guidance; seek the company of other Christ followers; endure until the suffering passes	Less health issues and injuries due to reckless behavior; less encounters with criminal justice system; able to comfort others with the lessons learned from this suffering

After we have a Biblical perspective on suffering, we can freely turn to God for relief. Psalm 23 depicts an important sequence of events where God first leads us to green pastures and still waters before we move on to facing the painful emotions of our past. We must be in a state of rest before we can safely return to the memories of when we were in the shadow of death. There is a reason why verses 2 and 3 in Psalm 23 highlight the importance of rest before we encounter verse 4, which says, "Even though I walk through the valley of the shadow of death, I will fear no evil, for You are with me" (Psalm 23:4, ESV).

Rest begins in our body. We can't revisit painful memories until we are calm in our bodies, resting in green pastures with our Shepherd. It can take quite a bit of work to feel calm and safe in our bodies. What does rest feel like in your body? When we are calm, we take long deep breaths. Our thoughts are not racing. Our muscles are relaxed. Sleep comes naturally. This state of peace is the next stop along our healing journey.

End of Chapter Reflection

Take a moment to journal through the following questions:

1) How have my beliefs about suffering affected my life?
2) How often do I relax?
3) How is my sleep these days?
4) What are my feelings about my body? Do I feel like it is a temple for the Holy Spirit, as described in 1 Corinthians 3:16?
5) Am I connected with my body?
6) Have I ever felt rested and calm in my body? If so, what did it feel like?
7) Have I used substances to achieve a temporary state of rest? If so, what were the pros and cons of this method?

CHAPTER 4: NEW PATHWAYS

God has built our bodies with a defense system of either fleeing, fighting, or freezing when there is danger. This defense system is constantly running in the background of our brains, scanning for danger and reacting subconsciously before we even have logical thoughts about it. For example, if a tiger entered your house, your logical brain would shut off and your unconscious defensive system would take over until the danger passes. Then your body would calm down again after you're safe.

We all react differently to dangerous situations and we all have different life experiences and resources that affect our responses. The choices our brain and nervous system make during horrific events are decisions we can't control. Our unconscious brain makes decisions about how to react in a split second, based on the resources we have and the details of the dangerous situation. Trauma occurs when our God-given coping system of flight, fight, or freeze isn't able to keep the danger away. Our brain has no plan for this and it just shuts down.

When our defense system wasn't adequate and we are harmed, our bodies become trapped in that moment when we felt helpless. Our bodies keep trying to complete the actions of fighting, fleeing, or freezing in order to fix the problem. The medical field has confirmed that many of us become stuck in this cycle after traumatic events.

This "stuck point" is the body trying to repair itself and it's a normal reaction. Many people find themselves stuck in various stages of fight, flight, of freeze even decades after traumatic events have occurred. Daniel Weiss, Ph.D created an assessment tool that helps us identify which defensive stages we are stuck in. He described elements of each stage in the "Impact of Event Scale." You will find a description of each stage on the charts below.

FIGHT

flashbacks with heart pounding, panic attacks, anxiety (sweating, trouble breathing, nausea, etc)
pictures about past events come into the mind without warning, waves of feeling like the event is happening now in the present
uncontrollable anger
finding yourself in relationships or situations where shouting and physical aggression may happen
feeling jumpy, on alert all the time for danger
trouble sleeping

Adapted from the IMPACT OF EVENT SCALE – REVISED by Daniel S. Weiss, Ph.D

FLIGHT

avoiding difficult emotions or sensations
avoiding letting oneself get upset when thinking about it or being reminded of it
a feeling that the trauma hadn't happened or wasn't real
staying away from reminders of it, trying to remove it from the memory, trying not to talk about it

Adapted from the IMPACT OF EVENT SCALE – REVISED by Daniel S. Weiss, Ph.D

FREEZE

spacing out
having few memories about the past
difficulty focusing
feeling numb with emotions and in your body
using substances and food to calm down the body and mind

Adapted from the IMPACT OF EVENT SCALE – REVISED by Daniel S. Weiss, Ph.D

Another word for the freeze response is "dissociating." This type of coping mechanism can keep us from feeling pain in the moment of trauma, but living in it keeps us from being in the present. It can also affect our ability to focus, our short term memory, and our ability to plan[8]. Dr. Ruth Lanius describes the effects of dissociation in this way:

"…we can have out-of-body experiences because things in our bodies can become so overwhelming that we have to detach from the emotions and the memories. People will often report that they look down on themselves from above because what they experience in their body is not tolerable for them anymore. Sometimes people will also report feeling that their hands or their feet are detached – again, in a way to detach themselves from their past experience and their intense emotions…dissociation can be so severe that the self fragments, and a person can feel like they have multiple selves because they can't carry all the intense emotions and all the intense memories in one state of consciousness – that would be way too overwhelming. So it gets separated and people can often feel very fragmented and feel that they don't have a sense of self." - Dr. Ruth Lanius[9]

The Window of Tolerance

Part of the healing process is to get "unstuck" from the constant state of living in the defensive stages of fight, flight, or freeze. The "Window of Tolerance'" is a concept developed by Dr. Dan Siegel. It describes the optimal state of being where, rather than living in a defensive stage, we find a more peaceful place where we can better manage our emotions, learn, play, and relate to ourselves and others[10]. This peaceful state is the "Window of Tolerance" that we strive for.

The first step towards expanding our window of tolerance is being aware of our body and how it feels in each stage. We must start with how our bodies feel in each state because our nervous system is the first to react when we feel threatened or scared. We can find ourselves in a defensive state before we even consciously realize what has happened.

The chart on the following page helps to describe the experience of moving back and forth between defensive stages and the window of tolerance. We will find healing as we become more aware of how often we move back and forth between these states of being. We can only ask for help when we are aware of what we are experiencing.

Different states of being can also be described as different levels of arousal. The highest arousal states we can be in are the defensive states of "fight" and "flight." These states are often described as being in "hyperarousal". Likewise, the lowest arousal state we can be in is the defensive state of "freeze." This is often called "hypoarousal." The window of tolerance is the optimal state of arousal where we are not too "hyper" or "hypo" aroused.

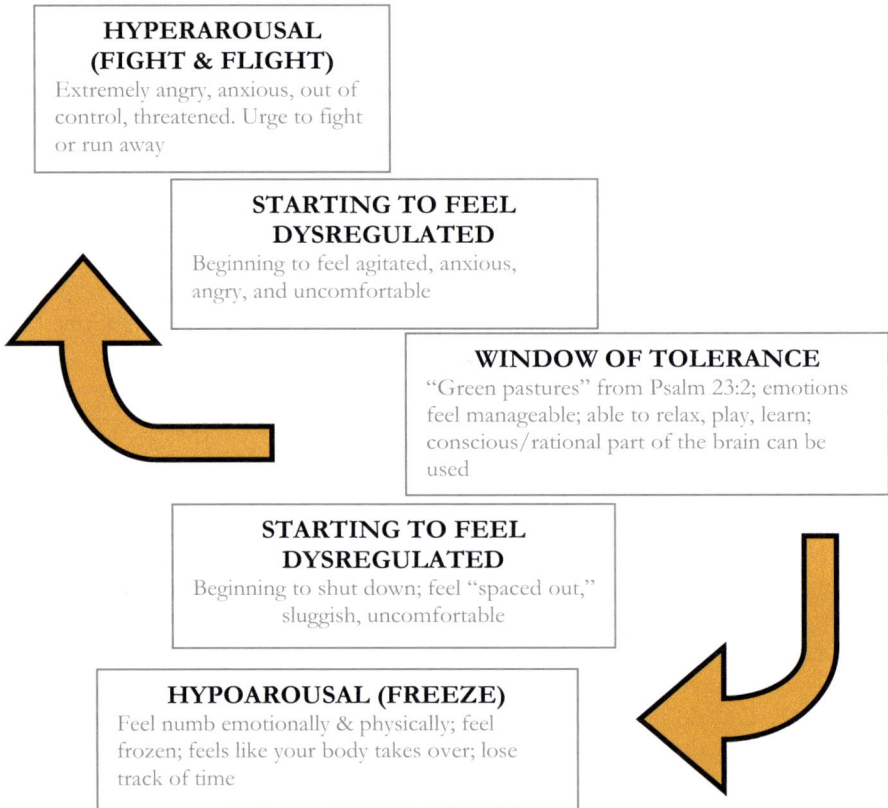

HYPERAROUSAL (FIGHT & FLIGHT)
Extremely angry, anxious, out of control, threatened. Urge to fight or run away

STARTING TO FEEL DYSREGULATED
Beginning to feel agitated, anxious, angry, and uncomfortable

WINDOW OF TOLERANCE
"Green pastures" from Psalm 23:2; emotions feel manageable; able to relax, play, learn; conscious/rational part of the brain can be used

STARTING TO FEEL DYSREGULATED
Beginning to shut down; feel "spaced out," sluggish, uncomfortable

HYPOAROUSAL (FREEZE)
Feel numb emotionally & physically; feel frozen; feels like your body takes over; lose track of time

Chart adapted from NICABM "How Trauma Can Affect Your Window of Tolerance"

God's design is that our bodies would move through these arousal states if we need to fight, flee, or freeze to survive and stay safe. When we sense a threat to our wellbeing, the unconscious part of our brain makes the decision to become hyper or hypo aroused based on the situation. Perhaps it's safer to fight or to play dead. If our defense system works and the danger passes without too much harm done to us, then our bodies relax and we return to the window of tolerance.

However, if our defense system is firing off and we are harmed anyway, our brain can't compute what just happened. Long after the traumatic event, our defense system operates like a broken electrical system. In everyday situations, it goes from all the way "on" (hyperarousal) to all the way "off" (hypoarousal), trying to fix the problem. Our body does not realize that the danger has passed. Most moments feel like a dangerous situation.

After trauma, our bodies become accustomed to snapping into states of hyper and hypo arousal. Our unconscious brain continues to call the shots and decides how we will feel. This process can make us feel like we're out of control. After an angry episode or a time period of zoning out, others may ask you, "Why did you do that?" You may say, "I don't know." Another way to explain why you don't know why you did what you did is, "My brain is so used to being hyper or hypo aroused that I just snapped into that state without choosing to."

The reason why we end up in angry or depressed states without choosing to is because our conscious brain is shut off during very high or very low states of arousal. God designed our brains this way because if we have to fight a tiger, we shouldn't be using brain cells to be rational and reasonable. All of our energy must go to survival. Likewise, if we must play dead to avoid pain, it will hurt much more if our conscious brain is online and is aware of what's happening.

Long after the tiger has gone away, our brain continues to live in these survival states. The key to being in your window of tolerance is to keep your conscious brain online. We do this by staying aware of our bodies and being conscious about what our body is doing. Over time, we become more familiar with our body cues and we can recognize when we are moving out of our window of tolerance and into dysregulation. After we are aware of what is happening, we can then learn to tolerate difficult emotions and uncomfortable body sensations without resorting to high or low arousal states.

Forming New Habits

Not only does it take time to become aware of our bodies, but it also takes time to build new neural pathways in our brains. Neural pathways are the paths of least resistance that neurons use to send signals to our brains about what to feel, eat, think, etc. They are the habits, unconscious thoughts, and knee-jerk reactions that we go to in order to function. They become like highways in our brains[11], establishing our everyday thoughts and actions.

Making changes is hard and God does not expect you to do it on your own strength. Psalm 23:3 says, "He leads me in paths of righteousness for His name's sake" (ESV). Just as this verse describes a Shepherd leading you down a path of righteousness, we can envision Jesus leading us down a new neural pathway in our brains. How is this done? When we feel our bodies shifting into a hyper or hypo arousal state, we can cry out, "Help!" and ask Jesus to enter this moment with us. In these moments, we want our conscious brain online and our spirit tuned in to the Holy Spirit. This will give us courage to allow the uncomfortable emotions to pass through us. Isaiah 43:19 says, "For I am about to do something new. See, I have already begun! Do you not see it? I will make a pathway through the wilderness" (NLT). You are not alone in this!

Staying Grounded

Another way to describe the window of tolerance is the feeling of being "grounded" or "present" no matter what is going on around you. Let's take a look at techniques for feeling grounded in our spirit, soul, and body.

Grounded in Your Spirit

Grounding Technique	Corresponding Bible Verse
Hearing Jesus' voice through prayer	"After He has gathered His own flock, He walks ahead of them, and they follow Him because they know His voice. They won't follow a stranger; they will run from him because they won't know his voice." John 10:4-5, NLT "Jesus replied, 'I am the bread of life. Whoever comes to Me will never be hungry again. Whoever believes in Me will never be thirsty.'" John 6:35, NLT
Feeding your spirit through God's Word	"But Jesus told him, 'No! The Scriptures say, People do not live by bread alone, but by every word that comes from the mouth of God.'" Matthew 4:4, NLT "For the word of God is alive and powerful. It is sharper than the sharpest two-edged sword, cutting between soul and spirit, between joint and marrow. It exposes our innermost thoughts and desires." Hebrews 4:12, NLT
Stopping negative self-talk with the Word of God	"We use God's mighty weapons, not worldly weapons, to knock

	down the strongholds of human reasoning and to destroy false arguments." 2 Corinthians 10:4, NLT "He canceled the record of the charges against us and took it away by nailing it to the cross. In this way, He disarmed the spiritual rulers and authorities. He shamed them publicly by His victory over them on the cross." Colossians 2:14-15, NLT "Search me, O God, and know my heart; test me and know my anxious thoughts. Point out anything in me that offends You, and lead me along the path of everlasting life." Psalm 139:23-24, NLT
Intentionally focusing on God's goodness by willing your mind to praise Him	"Bless the Lord, oh my soul, and all that is within me, bless His holy name! Bless the Lord, oh my soul, and forget not His benefits, who forgives all your iniquity, who heals all your diseases, who redeems your life from the pit, who crowns you with steadfast love and mercy, who satisfies you with good so that your youth is renewed like the eagle's." Psalm 103:1-5, ESV
Being free from mind-altering substances so you have mental clarity	"Don't be drunk with wine, because that will ruin your life. Instead, be filled with the Holy Spirit" Ephesians 5:18, NLT "Be sober-minded; be watchful. Your adversary the devil prowls around like a roaring lion, seeking someone to devour." 1 Peter 5:8, ESV
Allowing all emotions to pass through you, identifying their	"For God gave us a spirit not of fear but of power and love and self-

purpose and knowing they will pass	control" 2 Timothy 1:7, NLT
	"Be angry and do not sin" Ephesians 4:26, ESV
	"I know what it is to be in need, and I know what it is to have plenty. I have learned the secret of being content in any and every situation, whether well fed or hungry, whether living in plenty or in want. I can do all this through Him who gives me strength." Philippians 4:12-13, NIV

Grounded in Your Body

If body sensations become unbearable, distract yourself by counting to 10, look around and identify 3 things you can see, hear, and touch; or exercise. Start moving your body right in that moment.
Bring heart rate down and slow anger responses by taking long, deep breaths
Eat a balanced diet that fuels your body and mind

Now that we are becoming aware of our bodies and we have some grounding techniques, the next step is to explore the situations or thoughts that trigger our defense system to leave the window of tolerance. Sometimes you will find yourself in a state of hyper or hypo arousal and you will have no clue why your body and mind are reacting this way. This is because our unconscious defense system is constantly scanning our surroundings for threats. Our unconscious, survival brain may have interpreted something as a threat and it has already alerted your body to react. However, there are other triggers that we can consciously identify and begin reacting differently to.

As you begin to answer the questions on the following page, be sure to stop and use grounding techniques if you begin to feel overwhelming emotions. You may also want to explore these questions with a trusted friend next to you for support. Invite Jesus to lead you through these questions and give you insight.

TOUCH	What do I touch or who/what touches me that takes me out of my window of tolerance?
SIGHT	What do I see in the natural world or in my mind that takes me out of my window of tolerance?
SMELL	What do I smell that takes me out of my window of tolerance?
TASTE	What do I taste that takes me out of my window of tolerance?
HEAR	What do I hear from others or from myself in my head that takes me out of my window of tolerance?

End of Chapter Reflection

Take a moment to journal through the following questions:

1) When I have felt a threat to my wellbeing in the past, what defensive state did the unconscious part of my brain choose? (Fight, flight, or freeze)
2) Do I feel any resistance to becoming aware of my body?
3) How much time did I spend in each stage yesterday?
4) How does my body feel in each stage of survival (stomachache, headache, eyes becoming unfocused, etc)?
5) What would be some benefits of living in the window of tolerance more often?
6) How often do I ask Jesus for help when I'm moving out of my window of tolerance?
7) Am I ready to follow Jesus down new paths?
8) Do any fears spring up when I think about reaching for Jesus in these moments?

CHAPTER 5: REENACT

When our soul and body are stuck in a trauma response, we often find ourselves in situations where we are reliving the initial trauma in a different scenario. Because our defensive system was not able to prevent harm, our bodies continue to reenact the motions of fight, flight, or freeze in everyday life, hoping that these motions will protect us. What some would call self-destructive behaviors may actually be unconscious reenactments of the initial traumatic event. It is not uncommon for trauma survivors to question why further suffering and abuse seems to follow them wherever they go.

Dr. Ron Siegel explains this cycle in this way: "We may select people who are unsafe, for example –if we're used to unstable, unsafe people, that's what feels familiar, that's what we feel like we know how to connect to. Sometimes it's out of the wish to rework the problem: we had a volatile parent so we get a volatile romantic partner who we think is a little less volatile and maybe we can fix it this time[12]"

Before we explore how our past is affecting the ways we are behaving in the present, it is important to examine if our current environment is free from active danger. There is a difference between being stuck in a defensive response because of past trauma and having active defensive responses now because our current environment is not safe. Is your environment safe? Are you in any active, dangerous situations? If so, your body will not be able to rest in green pastures if your defensive system is constantly set to "ON" because the threat has not been removed. Will you allow Jesus to lead you down a path of safety where you can focus on your healing journey with Him? Reach out for help today and begin this new life of rest!

Exploring Our Reenactment Behaviors

If your environment does not have active danger in it, then it is useful to explore why we behave as if the danger is still hovering over us, about to reattack us at any time. One reason for this is that our brains continue to produce stress chemicals long after the traumatic event has passed[13]. Dr. Bessel van der Kolk says, "Trauma survivors are prone to continue the action, or rather the (futile) attempt at action, which began when the thing happened[14]".

For instance, if you weren't able to fight during the traumatic event, your body wants to continue the fighting defensive action in order to make it right. This may look like being prone to fighting at work or in relationships. If you were not able to run away during the traumatic event, your body may feel an urge to flee anytime you are in uncomfortable situations or you feel uncomfortable feelings. If you dissociated during the traumatic event, you may find yourself unable to be present when others have intense emotions around you. You may space out or fall asleep in these situations.

All of these reenactment behaviors put a strain on our relationships. The urge to fight, flee, or freeze was useful in the moment of trauma, but now these behaviors may be causing unwanted consequences in our lives.

What reenactment situations do you continuously find yourself in? How do these situations relate to the traumatic events in your past?

Reenactments with God

We can also find ourselves in reenactment situations with God. Do you find yourself fighting Him, running from Him, or tuning Him out? If so, how do these behaviors relate to the traumatic events in your life? Psalm 139:1-2 says, "O Lord, You have examined my heart and know everything about me. You know when I sit down or stand up. You know my thoughts even when I'm far away" (NLT). Will you follow Jesus down a new path of truth? He knows everything about you, you are perfect in His sight, and He is waiting for you.

Productive Reenactments

Trauma occurs when our defensive system was not able to keep us fully safe. Most trauma survivors were not able to fight back enough to stop the traumatic event. Your body can complete the defensive cycle of fighting that it wasn't able to complete by letting it do the motions of fighting back now, in the present. In order to do this, you have to find the place inside of you that wanted to fight back during the traumatic event. Even if your body was not able to fight, there might be another part of you that wanted to fight back[15]. Finding the defensive motions that set your body free will be a process that the Holy Spirit will lead you on.

As you begin this journey, consider these common productive reenactments that have worked for other trauma survivors:

✓ Self-defense class
✓ Running
✓ Boxing
✓ Weight Training
✓ Martial Arts
✓ Kickboxing

It is very important that you do not do these productive reenactments by yourself. As your body begins to fight, powerful emotions are often released. You will need the support of a trusted friend or a counselor as you embark on this empowerment phase of your journey. As intense feelings flow through your body, a safe person that you trust can help you stay in your window of tolerance by going through the process with you. You can keep your conscious brain online by talking through your experience. For instance, you can say, "My hands are shaking right now. My heart is pounding." You will also need to make use of grounding techniques during this time. While it has been useful for you to avoid uncomfortable feelings, this avoidance has also had some drawbacks. It is time to release your body and fight back.

Many trauma survivors report a sense of relief after engaging in these types of physical activities. They also report a growing ability to stay in the window of tolerance more often because the body is calmer after the emotional release.

End of Chapter Reflection

Take a moment to journal through the following questions:

1) When I make a timeline of my past relationships with others, is there a pattern of reenactment that relates to my trauma?
2) Do I have a part of me that wants to fight back and defend myself?

CHAPTER 6: ADAPT

We will now explore the self-soothing techniques we have turned to in response to the overwhelming emotions that course through our bodies every day. To review, those intense emotions continue to course through us long after the traumatic event because our defensive systems are permanently set to "ON", which results in toxic stress, hyperarousal, and depression.

As part of God's design for the family, our caregivers are supposed to soothe us when we are young. We do not naturally know how to calm down when we cry or when we need food. We learn how to soothe ourselves after our caregivers meet our needs.

As young children, many of us had to adapt to our surroundings when we weren't always soothed by our caregivers. We may have turned to food, or sleep, or media to numb our anxiety and fill in the gaps where we weren't nurtured enough.

Although God's design was for our caregivers to build us up in early childhood, the reality of sin is that we were all raised by imperfect adults. As a result, everyone has gaps in their development and we all have turned to other things instead of Jesus. A normal part of adult life is learning to be satisfied with Jesus, not looking to other things for love and acceptance.

Self-Soothing Crisis

After we experience traumatic events, our self-soothing system is shattered. We leave the normal adult experience of filling in the gaps with Jesus and enter a nightmare where our bodies feel out of control and nothing seems to soothe us enough to even hear God's voice. When our defensive systems are permanently set to "ON", we constantly go through gut-wrenching and heart-breaking sensations in our bodies[16].

Dr. Bessel van der Kolk says, "If you have these sensations as an adult, you try to do something to make it go away. You may take Prozac or you may go to the gym, or you may get drunk, or you may have sex with a stranger – something to manage those bodily systems[17]." He also describes a common self-soothing cycle where the goal is to dissociate and feel nothing, so when troubling feelings come up, trauma survivors will cut themselves or use drugs to get back to that numb state again[18].

The self-soothing cycle depicted in this chart below can cause havoc in our lives, yet it continues to happen because we do not know how to soothe ourselves in the midst of such intense feelings. Let's examine this cycle further and identify the external self-soothing techniques we have used.

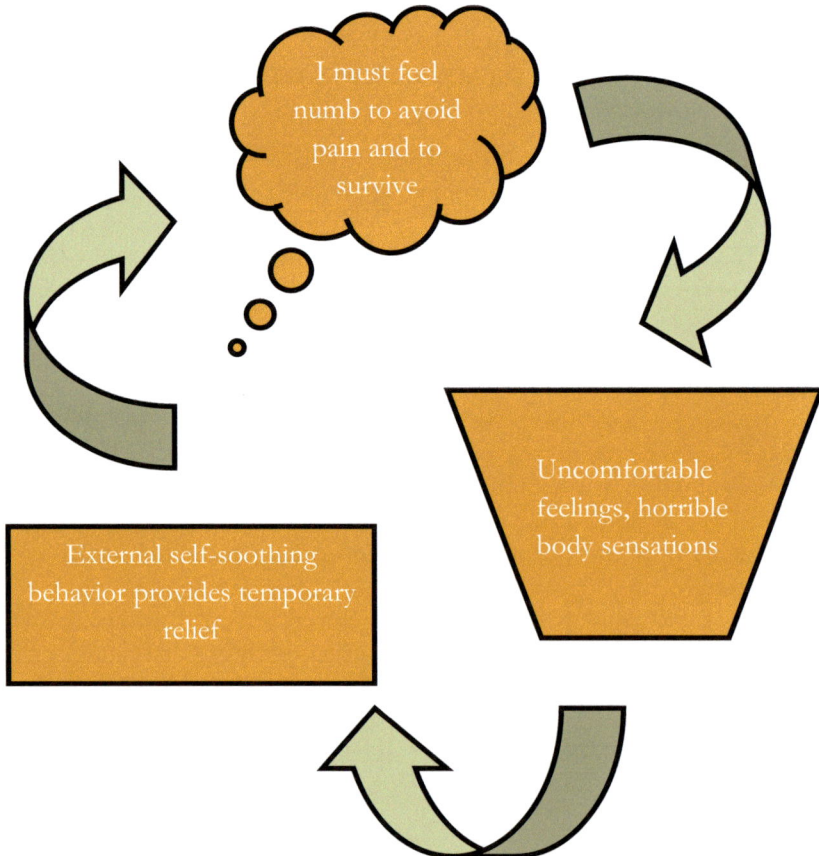

I must feel numb to avoid pain and to survive

Uncomfortable feelings, horrible body sensations

External self-soothing behavior provides temporary relief

Have you found yourself in this cycle before? If so, what external self-soothing behaviors have you been drawn to? Many people report turning to food, substances, self-mutilation, or needing constant reassurance from others. Others have turned to "people pleasing" behavior to gain acceptance from others.

Breaking the Cycle

Breaking the cycle starts with restoring the link between your body and emotions. We must feel ok inside our bodies or we will continue to self-soothe with external things[19]. Dr. Bessel van der Kolk describes why it is so hard to feel ok inside of ourselves: "Traumatized people chronically feel unsafe inside their bodies: The past is alive in the form of gnawing interior discomfort. They often become expert at ignoring their gut feelings and in becoming numb. People who cannot comfortably notice what is going on inside respond to any sensory shift either by shutting down or by going into a panic—they develop a fear of fear itself. The price for ignoring or distorting the body's messages is being unable to detect what is truly dangerous or harmful for you and, just as bad, what is safe or nourishing. They tend to register emotions as physical problems rather than as signals that something deserves their attention. Instead of feeling angry or sad, they experience muscle pain, bowel irregularities, or other symptoms for which no cause can be found[20]."

Repairing the Self-Regulation System

If we are numbing all of our feelings, this means that we're also blocking the feelings that let us decide what is dangerous or safe. We also block out the ability to feel pleasure. After trauma, we do not trust ourselves to decide or feel anything.

After we become more aware of our bodies and emotions, the next step is to restore our self-regulation system. This self-regulation system can detect what we are feeling and decide which self-soothing behavior to use to make us feel better. When this system is restored, we feel in control of ourselves again. We feel confident that we can care for ourselves and be proactive in meeting our needs.

As we follow Jesus and allow Him to restore our souls (Psalm 23:3), the self-soothing crisis cycle on the previous page can be transformed into a healthy self-regulation system, found on the next page.

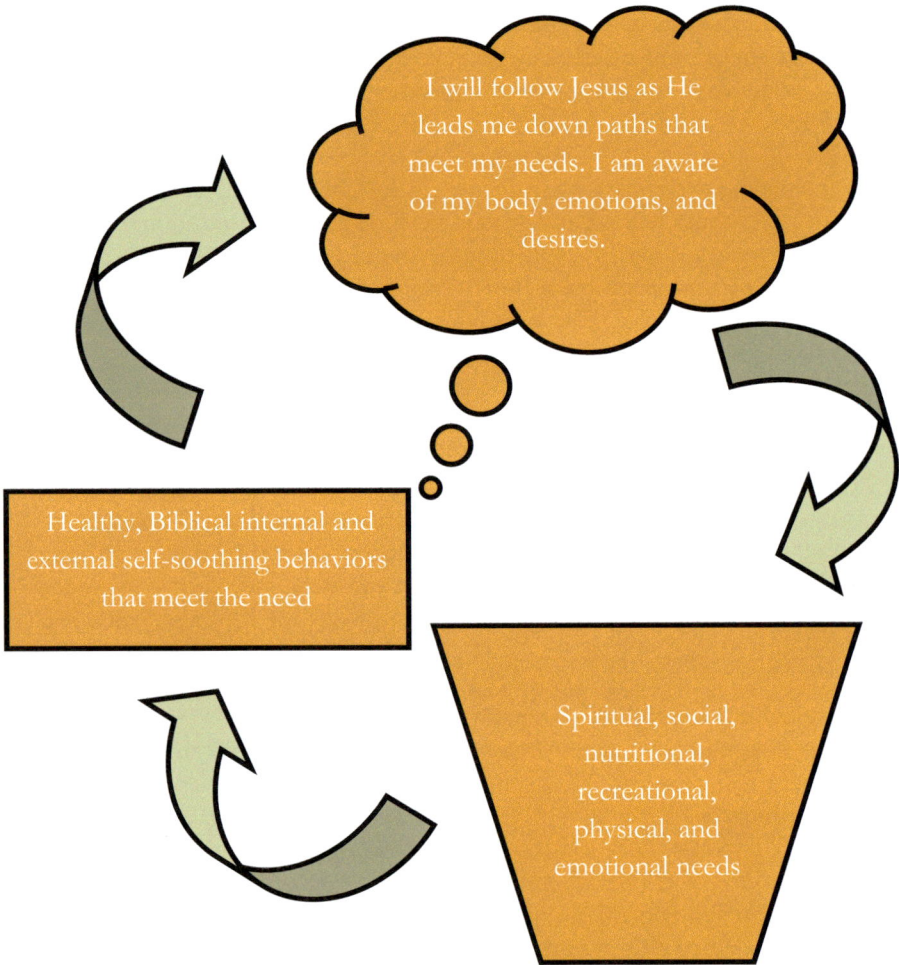

I will follow Jesus as He leads me down paths that meet my needs. I am aware of my body, emotions, and desires.

Healthy, Biblical internal and external self-soothing behaviors that meet the need

Spiritual, social, nutritional, recreational, physical, and emotional needs

Soul Check In

Many trauma survivors struggle with this stage of healing. It can be difficult to voice our own needs and desires. We can feel doubtful that there are better solutions than the self-soothing behaviors we have been using for so long. Let's review how God heals us and produces change.

First He calls us to Himself, then He protects and loves us. Do you feel like you are His loved, protected child? As a reminder of your special position as His favored, perfect child, read these verses in Isaiah 41 and write your name in the blank.

"But you, _____, My servant, _____, whom I have chosen, the offspring of Abraham, My friend; you whom I took from the ends of the earth and called from its farthest corners, saying to you, _____, "You are My servant, I have chosen you and not cast you off;" fear not for I AM with you; be not dismayed, for I AM your God; I will strengthen you, I will help you, I will uphold you with My righteous right hand. Behold, all who are incensed against you shall be put to shame and confounded; those who strive against you shall be as nothing and shall perish." Isaiah 41:8-11, ESV

It is only in this safe place of protection with God that God begins to repair us. You don't have to know how He will repair your self-regulation system. It is a process that requires us to believe that our needs come from God and we are important enough that He will help us fill them.

End of Chapter Reflection

Take a moment to journal through the following questions:
1) Do I believe that Jesus can help me find ways to meet my needs?
2) What are my needs and desires?
3) What are some self-soothing behaviors that my spirit needs? Soul? Body?

CHAPTER 7: ACCEPT

One of the hardest paths to follow Jesus on is the path to accepting how our bodies reacted during times of intense stress and trauma. It is not your fault that someone sinned against you and your body went into defense mode. There are things that happen in this fallen world that are so horrific that our survival, unconscious brain steps in and takes over. In the moment of a traumatic event, we shut down and go into crisis mode. This is an unconscious decision and it's not a moral thing. Our bodies try to protect us, but sometimes our resources aren't enough to cope with such dreadful events.

Luckily, we are not ruled by our bodies or our souls, which are susceptible to damage. We are ruled by the Holy Spirit living in us, who is perfect and able to heal. We are damaged, yet He is whole. He speaks to our spirit, which restores our souls, and in turn, heals our bodies.

Our defense system will continue to go off throughout our lives until Jesus returns and wipes every tear from our eyes and takes away all pain. While we wait for His return in this fallen world, the way to safety is to let Jesus meet you where you are crawled up in a ball and lead you out of crisis mode every time. When our bodies make the decision to shut down, we call on Him to restore us back to safety.

Preparing to Face the Truth
The following reflection questions may be very difficult to answer. Be

sure to have your grounding techniques available for your spirit, soul, and body. Answer these questions with a trusted friend or counselor. Do not answer them alone. If you feel yourself leaving the window of tolerance, keep your conscious brain online by describing your bodily sensations as they pass through you. Rely on your support system and the strength of the Holy Spirit.

Reflection Exercise

1) What sensations go through your body when you read this statement?

   "It is not my fault that someone sinned against me and my body unconsciously decided how to react. During that moment of terror, my conscious brain was completely turned off and my unconscious, survival brain was making the decisions. God does not hold me accountable for how I reacted in that moment."

2) What thoughts does your mind think when you read the statement above?

3) Do you blame yourself for shutting down or not having the resources to cope during a traumatic event? This blame is not from Jesus and you are released from this.

4) If you were a child when someone sinned against you, do you blame yourself for not fighting back or freezing? We are wired for community and we are desperate for relationships. Forgive yourself for tolerating a corrupted option because it was one of the only ways to get your needs met. Accept that you were a small, defenseless child and the way your unconscious brain chose to react was a calculation for survival.

5) Sometimes, shaming and blaming ourselves feels more in control than admitting that we felt powerless in those traumatic moments. How did shaming yourself help you? How is it harming you now?

6) Do you have condemning thoughts such as, "If I'm a Christian, why didn't I just find God's peace right away? Why didn't I react the "right" way?" If so, that is not from God. Instead, He says that no matter what has happened in your past, "There is now no condemnation for those who are in Christ Jesus" Romans 8:1, NIV.

7) How does your body feel right now? Any tension, discomfort, pain, etc? What emotions are you feeling right now?

Let's return to the chart that provides a snapshot of how we create meaning from events that have happened to us. The first chart below illustrates false beliefs that we often tell ourselves. The second chart on the following page provides the real truth about what happened, according to the Bible.

Event	Belief	Emotion	Behavior	Consequences
Any event or circumstance that impacts us; Events that affected how we adapted and protected ourselves (may or may not have a specific memory of it)	*How we interpret events. Always comes before an emotion. Formed from our environments growing up. How did we learn about emotions from family, culture, etc?*	*What we feel* *4 Core Emotions: Anger, Fear, Sadness, Happiness*	*What we do*	*The external events that occur as a result of our behavior*
Someone sinned against me and violated my body, emotions, and needs	[False beliefs] My reaction made it worse. I should've handled it better. The other person probably chose me to sin against because I am damaged or bad. False acceptance in the form of "I deserved it. God was punishing me."	Shame, Guilt, Blaming myself, Intense self-hatred	Ignoring or despising my needs, punishing myself through self-sabotaging behavior	Difficult to maintain healthy relationships with boundaries and equal "give" and "take" Isolated from God Isolated from others

Chart is adapted from Albert Ellis' ABC Model & Brenda Cochran's Whole Person Framework Theory

BIBLICAL WORLDVIEW OF TRAUMA

Event	Belief	Emotion	Behavior	Consequences
Someone sinned against me and violated my body, emotions, and needs	God knew exactly how my unconscious brain was going to react to this horrific event. He made my brain and He is not blaming me for that. As it was happening, He already had the plan to lead me to complete restoration and healing. He has defeated sin and death and He shares that victory with me even while I am on this earth and He hasn't returned yet.	Deep sadness and grief, crying out to God for relief and healing, righteous anger at the injustice done to me	Waiting on God to heal me. Holding Him to His promises and asking Him for it every day, with faith that He will come.	A painful path of healing that results in joy and the ability to comfort others as they go down a similar path towards healing.

Chart is adapted from Albert Ellis' ABC Model & Brenda Cochran's Whole Person Framework Theory

End of Chapter Reflection

Take a moment to journal through the following questions:

1) Which chart do I identify with the most right now? Why?
2) Do I often blame myself for the actions of others?

CHAPTER 8: GRIEVE

Psalm 23:4 says, "Even though I walk through the valley of the shadow of death, I will fear no evil for You are with me" (ESV). Since this verse says "*I walk*," we may interpret that as "I walked through the valley of the shadow of death" so it was my choice to enter this valley of death and it was my fault. As we have covered, it was not your choice that someone else sinned against you, and we are not to blame for the way our defensive system responded in that time of danger.

When we begin the process of accepting that it wasn't our fault when someone sinned against us, we often start to wonder, "Then whose fault was it?" If I was walking through the valley of the shadow of death and I didn't choose to, then who pushed me into that valley? Why was I there?

In chapter three, we explored the idea of suffering and concluded that it comes from sin. We discussed how sin is the cause of suffering because the Bible shows us the beauty of God's created world before sin entered the picture and it tells us about the pain-free existence we will have when Jesus returns. When God creates an environment, it reflects His goodness, love, and joy. We also explored the effects of sin in chapter one. Where God's presence produces life, sin produces death. Sin causes evil, hate, and pain.

Active Grief

When we are in active grief, these words can sound hollow. We can read the words on the page, but they don't feel real. Psalm 23:4 says, "for You are with me." When we are grieving, we need to feel God is tangibly with us in a way that overwhelms our soul and body. When we are in the valley of the shadow of death, we need Him to show up in a powerful way.

The good news is that grief is God's specialty. When we realize that grief has been at the root of our emotional experiences, we will find that God is willing and ready to meet us in our grief. This part of your healing journey is very personal between you and Jesus. If you are beginning a stage of grief about the valley of the shadow of death that you walked through or are currently walking through, allow the grieving emotions to flow through you so that you can receive God's healing.

Matthew 5:4 (NLT) says that "God blesses those who mourn, for they will be comforted." 2 Corinthians 1:3 (NLT) says, "God is our merciful Father and the source of all comfort." He will meet us right where we are at in our emotional state and He will bring peace and comfort. He is not afraid of our questions or doubts.

God's Healing Process: CPR

In chapter two, we learned how God's healing process follows a pattern. He first (C)ALLS us, then (P)ROTECTS us, then (R)EPAIRS us. When we come to God with our grief, we are heart broken and we need to be repaired. We trust that He has called us and we are saved by His grace. We know that He is our protector and He is not the cause of our suffering. Now we can trust Him to repair those broken places hidden inside of us. Just how does He repair our deepest hurts?

He heals us supernaturally, from His spirit to our spirit. His Spirit will deliver Jesus' words to us in a powerful way that is unique to what we need. John 14:26 (NLT) says, "But when the Father sends the Advocate as My representative—that is, the Holy Spirit—He will teach you everything and will remind you of everything I have told you." Paul explains the process in Romans 8:26-27 (NLT), which says, "And the Holy Spirit helps us in our weakness. For example, we don't know what God wants us to pray for. But the Holy Spirit prays for us with groanings that cannot be expressed in words. And the Father who knows all hearts knows what the Spirit is saying, for the Spirit pleads for us believers in harmony with God's own will."

There will be transforming moments where He alleviates your heaviest grief with His Spirit. You may still experience grief at different moments, but you will be able to return to those insights and reach out to Him for comfort again and again. This intimacy with Him becomes a process that produces peace and healing in our souls and bodies. Until He returns and fully restores this world, He heals us bit by bit, from glory to glory, again and again.

2 Corinthians 3:18 (NLT) says, "So all of us who have had that veil removed can see and reflect the glory of the Lord. And the Lord—who is the Spirit—makes us more and more like Him as we are changed into His glorious image."

Here is a road map of how God walks through the valley of the shadow of death with us and brings us out to the other side. He MENDS our soul during the repairing process by leading us to (M) meditate on His Word, (E) expect He will come, (N) narrate our expectation, (D) delay until He comes, and (S) speak about His deliverance.

(M) Meditate on God's Word

In our grief, we have intense emotions and desperate questions for God, such as "Why did this happen?" and "Where were You?" God will answer through His Word. The answers and the comfort that we need will come from the Bible, so we must begin to meditate on it. As we read His promises of healing and comfort, we probably won't feel healed or comforted yet. It's ok to be honest with God and say, "I see this promise in Your Word, but it doesn't feel true right now." Even in the absence of feeling, we can acknowledge that God's word is still true.

How can we meditate on Bible verses? We can write them down again and again. We can think about them as we're doing errands and going through our day. Deuteronomy 6:7-9 (NLT) says, "Repeat them again and again to your children. Talk about them when you are at home and when you are on the road, when you are going to bed and when you are getting up. Tie them to your hands and wear them on your forehead as reminders. Write them on the doorposts of your house and on your gates."

Let's do an example together. Suppose we read Isaiah 61:3 (NLT) where God promises, "To all who mourn in Israel, He will give a crown of beauty for ashes, a joyous blessing instead of mourning, festive praise instead of despair. In their righteousness, they will be like great oaks that the Lord has planted for His own glory." We might pray, *"God, I am grieving right now. I only feel the ashes. I do not have a crown of beauty. I don't feel Your joyous blessing right now. I am in despair. I do not have praise to give right now. I don't know how You will get through to me, but I ask You to pursue me and make Your promises true to me. I will wait for You."*

You may want to spend some time journaling to God and telling Him what the ashes feel like. We need to be honest, yet put our hope in His promises. See the "Promises to Meditate On" chart at the end of this chapter for verses about God's healing power. These verses are excellent ones to meditate on daily as you wait for your healing.

(E) Expect He Will Come

After you have identified the promises that you are putting your hope in, the next step is to wait in eager anticipation for the Lord to move in this area of your life. The promises that He made about healing are true. He will come with insight and comfort. Your assurance that He's going to do it is not based on your efforts, but on who He is and your position as His child. We can pray for healing and appeal to God's faithfulness. It's not on you to heal yourself, it's on God. He said the Holy Spirit will deliver His truth to you. Like a daughter who asks her father for something, don't be afraid to call on God to do what He said He would do in His word. He ALWAYS comes through because His word is true and He is faithful. Here are some verses about waiting for the Lord to rescue us:

Hebrews 11:1 ESV "Now faith is the assurance of things hoped for, the conviction of things not seen."

Isaiah 35:3-4 (ESV) "Strengthen the weak hands, and make firm the feeble knees. Say to those who have an anxious heart, "Be strong; fear not! Behold, your God will come with vengeance, with the recompense of God. He will come and save you."

Proverbs 30:5 ESV "Every word of God proves true; He is a shield to those who take refuge in Him."

Psalm 57:2-3 ESV "I cry out to God most high, to God who fulfills His purpose for me. He will send from Heaven and save me. He will put to shame him who tramples on me."

(N) Narrate Our Expectation

Part of stepping out in faith is telling others that you're believing it will happen before God delivers you. It's good for us to tell others that we don't feel the healing yet, but we are meditating on His Word and waiting for Him. It is very important to note that we cannot grieve alone. It is a community process. Galations 6:2 (NIV) says, "Carry each other's burdens, and in this way you will fulfill the law of Christ." Romans 12:15 commands us to "Rejoice with those who rejoice, weep with those who weep" (ESV). We need others to carry our burden as we call on God and ask Him to comfort us. All too often, we are tempted to isolate when we are in grief. It's hard to be vulnerable and admit we are walking through the valley of death. Who is your support team? Who can grieve with you? Who can hold onto God's promises for you when you are having a really bad day?

(D) Delay Until He Comes

We must follow God's timeline for healing. It does us no good to rush the process and move on before we actually hear from God. Wait for God to deliver His promise to you with His Holy spirit. You will know when it happens because His Word will come alive in that moment. The promise will become real to you. You will receive insights about yourself and how God is working in your life. God is very creative. He will deliver His truth in a variety of ways. Maybe through a sermon, a song, a verse, something someone else said about Him, etc. Don't compare your journey with someone else's. Just keep repeating steps 1-3 (Meditate, Expect, Narrate) and He will come on His own timing. Many people give up during this time and stop expecting God to heal them. Don't give up!

(S) Speak About His Deliverance

After God has met you in your darkest hour and He has delivered His Word to you, it's now time to testify and share your story. Psalm 9:13-14 (NLT) says, "Lord, have mercy on me. See how my enemies torment me. Snatch me back from the jaws of death. Save me so I can praise you publicly at Jerusalem's gates, so I can rejoice that You have rescued me." After God has healed our deepest wounds, we can then comfort others who are going through the same thing. 1 Corinthians 1:4 (NLT) says, "He comforts us in all our troubles so that we can comfort others. When they are troubled, we will be able to give them the same comfort God has given us."

PROMISES TO MEDITATE ON
Psalm 107:13-14 ESV "Then they cried to the Lord in their trouble, and He delivered them from their distress. He brought them out of darkness and the shadow of death and burst their bonds apart."
Psalm 119:50 ESV "This is my comfort in my affliction, that Your promise gives me life."
John 16:33 ESV "I have said these things to you, that in Me you may have peace. In the world you have tribulation. But take heart; I have overcome the world."
Jeremiah 17:7-8 ESV "Blessed is the man who trusts in the Lord, whose trust is the Lord. He is like a tree planted by water, that sends out its roots by the stream, and does not fear when heat comes, for its leaves remain green, and is not anxious in the year of drought, for it does not cease to bear fruit."
Psalm 31:7-8 ESV "I will rejoice and be glad in Your steadfast love, because You have seen my affliction, You have known the distress of my soul, and You have not delivered me into the hand of the enemy."
Isaiah 32:18 ESV "My people will abide in a peaceful habitation, in secure dwellings, and in quiet resting places."
Psalm 147:3 ESV "He heals the brokenhearted and binds up their wounds."
Isaiah 40:11 ESV "He will tend His flock like a shepherd; He will gather the lambs in His arms; He will carry them in His bosom, and gently lead

those that are with young."
Zephaniah 3:17 ESV "The Lord your God is in your midst, a mighty one who will save; He will rejoice over you with gladness; He will quiet you by His love; He will exult over you with loud singing."
Proverbs 3:24-26 ESV "If you lie down, you will not be afraid; when you lie down, your sleep will be sweet. Do not be afraid of sudden terror or of the ruin of the wicked, when it comes, for the Lord will be your confidence and will keep your foot from being caught."
Deuteronomy 1:30-31 ESV "The Lord your God who goes before you will Himself fight for you, just as He did for you in Egypt before your eyes, and in the wilderness, where you have seen how the Lord your God carried you, as a man carries His son, all the way that you went until you came to this place."

End of Chapter Reflection

Take a moment to journal through the following questions:

1) Which method of scripture meditation do I prefer? (Journaling, speaking it out loud, listening to audio, etc.)
2) What holds me back from meditating on God's Word?

CHAPTER 9: SAFETY

To understand why our bodies get stuck after a traumatic event, let's take a look at the type of situation where our bodies do not get stuck. Your body usually recovers from danger when your defense system worked and the harm was avoided or reduced. This is called "orientation trauma[21]." In this case, the body recovers and life moves on.

Orientation Trauma Chart

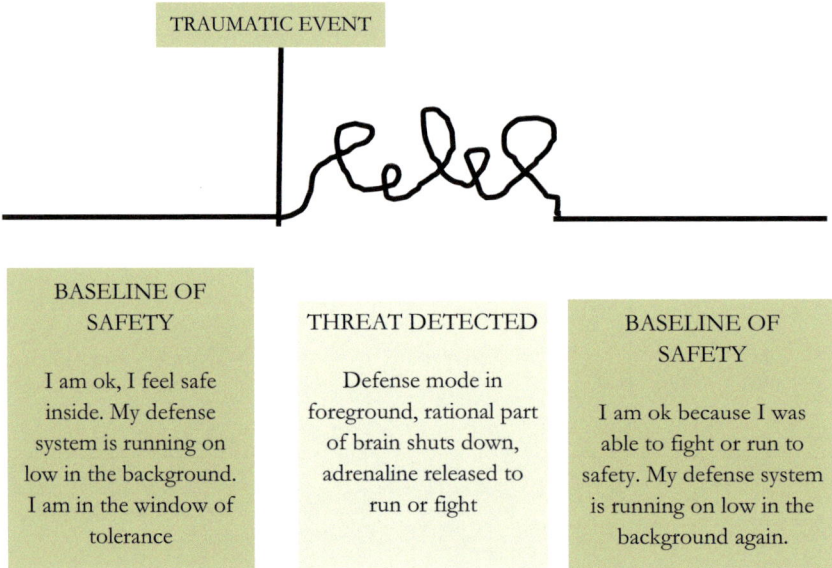

TRAUMATIC EVENT

BASELINE OF SAFETY	THREAT DETECTED	BASELINE OF SAFETY
I am ok, I feel safe inside. My defense system is running on low in the background. I am in the window of tolerance	Defense mode in foreground, rational part of brain shuts down, adrenaline released to run or fight	I am ok because I was able to fight or run to safety. My defense system is running on low in the background again.

Acute Trauma

When we try to fight and the person is bigger than us, or we try to flee and we are caught, or we try to freeze and play dead, but the trauma keeps happening to our bodies anyway, our defense systems completely fail us and our bodies get completely stuck. If you had a baseline of safety before the traumatic event, it may have felt like your world was turned upside down after the trauma occurred. Starting from a baseline of safety and then having it shattered is experiencing "single event trauma" or "acute trauma"[22]. Examples of acute trauma could be sexual or physical assault, a car accident, a painful medical experience or injury, sudden or violent loss of a loved one, or witnessing violence[23].

Many people find that their worldview changes after they have gone through acute trauma. We began to ask, "Am I safe?" "Can others be trusted?" In addition, our defensive systems turn to the "ON" setting all of the time. Even though keeping the defense system stuck to ON all the time is our body's natural reaction to trauma, it becomes a cycle that doesn't produce healing. Our bodies weren't meant to be using this much of our defense system all the time, so our body reacts with inflammation and immune system issues such as: rheumatoid arthritis, psoriasis, Crohn's disease, celiac disease, lupus, and many other bodily symptoms. Prolonged stress on the body also can lead to heart disease, diabetes, substance use, etc.

Recovery from acute trauma involves getting back to the baseline of safety that the survivor once had before the traumatic event occurred. This is not an easy task. One of the reasons why we can't easily return to our baseline of safety after acute trauma is because the world looks different now. After a single event trauma, we feel that we've learned something few others seem to be acknowledging. We aren't safe and maybe we never were. We can feel angry at others for not being as aware of this as we are because now our bodies are constantly in this reality. How can others be relaxed and laughing when danger could happen at any time? How was I once so relaxed when the world is such a dark place?

Suffering Changes Us

When you go through suffering, you become a different person. After a traumatic event, your personality is altered. Different genes are activated to respond to this new environment. Our bodies go through stress that we weren't meant to have. Our brains rearrange themselves to accommodate all the watchfulness and constant fear. We learn all too well that we aren't safe now, and maybe we never were. Our bodies are crying out, *this isn't right! Something is wrong!*

A New Baseline of Safety

When our bodies and souls calm down after acute trauma, our baseline of safety won't look the same as it did before the trauma. We are changed from the intense agony we have walked through. Healing will produce a new type of safety that knows how to find healing from suffering when life gets hard.

Acute Trauma Chart

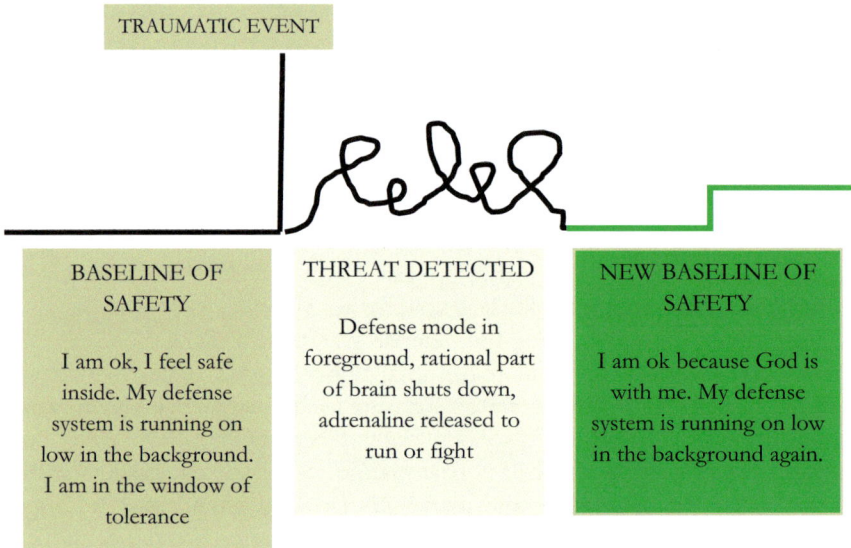

TRAUMATIC EVENT

BASELINE OF SAFETY	THREAT DETECTED	NEW BASELINE OF SAFETY
I am ok, I feel safe inside. My defense system is running on low in the background. I am in the window of tolerance	Defense mode in foreground, rational part of brain shuts down, adrenaline released to run or fight	I am ok because God is with me. My defense system is running on low in the background again.

Complex Trauma

Another type of trauma is when no baseline of safety was established. We go from one trauma to another throughout life, starting in early childhood. The goal is to establish a completely new baseline of safety that has never happened before.

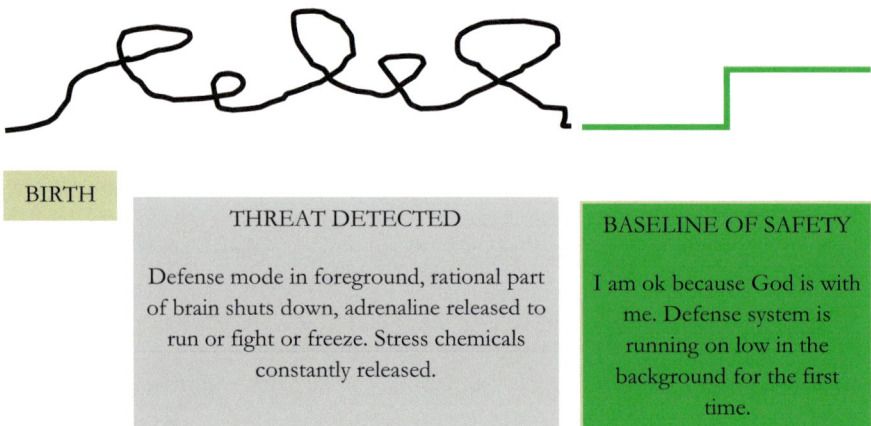

BIRTH

THREAT DETECTED	BASELINE OF SAFETY
Defense mode in foreground, rational part of brain shuts down, adrenaline released to run or fight or freeze. Stress chemicals constantly released.	I am ok because God is with me. Defense system is running on low in the background for the first time.

48

The Impacts of Childhood Trauma

Childhood trauma is when a child did not have enough safety to live in the window of tolerance while growing up. To review, the window of tolerance is when our emotions feel manageable, we can relax, we can play and learn, and our conscious, rational brain is being used most of the time. If there was enough danger that we were on alert most of the time during our childhood, our brains made adjustments so we could survive. For instance, our brains wanted to keep us safe, so more stress hormones were secreted, which allowed us to be alert at all times and to be ready to run or fight[24]. Unfortunately, this constant stress response interferes with the development of our conscious, rational brain where we can use reason and think through our decisions[25]. Let's take a look at the picture below, which shows the difference between a child who has been nurtured by a caregiver and a child who has been emotionally and physically neglected.

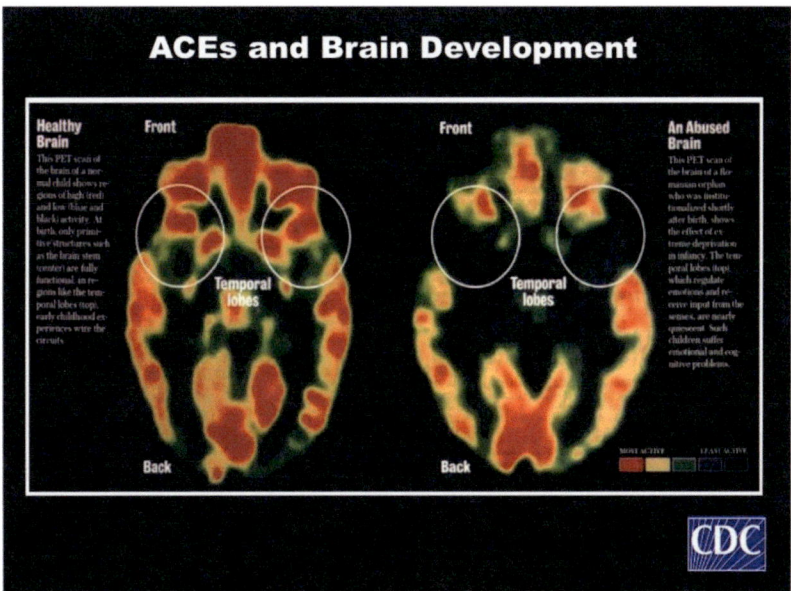

Photo from CDC, retrieved from
https://www.nea.org/sites/default/files/styles/1520wide/public/2020-07/ACEs_BrainDevelopment_MRI_Image.png?itok=oME46Jd6

When we are young, our brain develops from the bottom up[26]. In other words, it first develops our unconscious brain that's focused on survival. Once that is established, our conscious, rational part of our brain begins to develop, which is the part of the brain that is able to plan ahead and comprehend abstract thinking[27].

Just how does this development happen? The brain develops by forming social connections[28]. These crucial relationships come from our caregivers[29]. As we express our needs as infants and our caregivers meet our needs consistently, our brain connections become stronger[30]. As our brains become confident that our caregivers will allow us to survive, more social connections are built and our brain is able to develop the higher-level-thinking areas of our brains.

God created us to be very social beings. We are born defenseless and we cannot soothe ourselves. God charges parents with meeting their children's needs so that the child can eventually develop a conscious, rational part of the brain that can respond to His Word and become His child. Once we are older and we have developed complex thinking and logic, we can understand who God is and begin our journey of having Him as our perfect Father.

In a perfect world, we would learn that our needs are important from the consistent care of our parents. We would learn to soothe ourselves little by little by how our parents soothed us. We would cry, get fed, and stop crying. Unfortunately, we don't live in a perfect world. Not all of our needs were met when we were young and our brains were still developing. Some of our parents delivered us into our adolescence with a belief that we were safe and the ability to live in the window of tolerance. And some of our parents delivered us into adolescence with a belief that we were not safe and we needed to protect ourselves at all costs.

End of Chapter Reflection

Take a moment to journal through the following questions:

1. Do you still feel like you're in the valley of the shadow of death?
2. Do you feel safe at this point in your life?
3. Would you say you had a baseline of safety growing up?

CHAPTER 10: CONNECT

It is not too late to form a brand new baseline of safety or to restore a baseline of safety because Your perfect, powerful Father has everything you need to thrive in this fallen world. Where your earthly parents fell short, God will fill in the gaps. Where your family of origin missed the mark, your church family can come alongside you and provide belonging and acceptance. God gives us all the same grace and He will not leave you lacking. Whether we had good enough parents who met most of our needs, or if we had parents who did not meet our needs, God calls us all to the same two tasks once we become believers: (1) make God our Father and (2) connect with our brothers and sisters in Christ. Let's examine both areas more closely.

Make God Our Father

In Luke 14:26-27, Jesus says some shocking things about our families. He says, "If you want to be My disciple, you must, by comparison, hate everyone else—your father and mother, wife and children, brothers and sisters—yes, even your own life. Otherwise, you cannot be My disciple. And if you do not carry your own cross and follow Me, you cannot be my disciple" (NLT). Our identity, our allegiance, and our orders must come from God, our Father. If we will let Him, He will guide our life with the protective wisdom of a father.

Psalm 23:4 paints a picture of how Jesus, our Shepherd, guides us each day. It says, "Your rod and Your staff protect and comfort me" (ESV). A shepherd uses rods and staffs to guide the sheep into safety[31]. The shepherd may also use the rod to fight off any wild animals trying to attack his sheep.

The Bible also compares a rod to discipline. Hebrews 12:5-8 says, "And have you forgotten the encouraging words God spoke to you as His children? He said, 'My child, don't make light of the Lord's discipline, and don't give up when He corrects you. For the Lord disciplines those He loves, and He punishes each one He accepts as His child.' As you endure this divine discipline, remember that God is treating you as His own children. Who ever heard of a child who is never disciplined by its father? If God doesn't discipline you as He does all of His children, it means that you are illegitimate and are not really His children at all" (NLT).

This passage in Hebrews makes perfect sense if you had reasonable parents who had consistent expectations and the discipline was fair and understandable. Discipline includes training and teaching, not unpredictable outbursts or harsh abuse. Ephesians 6:4 says, "Fathers, do not provoke your children to anger by the way you treat them. Rather, bring them up with the discipline and instruction that comes from the Lord" (NLT). It can be hard to accept God's loving discipline when our earthly parents did not use loving discipline. Ask God to help you redefine the meanings of "discipline," "Father," and any other discrepancies that arise between your earthly parents and God, your Father.

If you did not have a baseline of safety established during your childhood, it may be useful to unpack more details about abuse or neglect that was done to you. These early experiences leave an impression on us and the thought patterns and adaptations we made in those early years may be hindering us from enjoying the love and discipline from God, your Father.

Connecting With Brothers & Sisters in Christ

Whether you are close with your family of origin or not, God calls us to make new bonds with our family of believers. Jesus made it clear that our fellow believers should truly be considered our family members. Matthew 12:46-50 (NLT) says, "While Jesus was still talking to the crowd, His mother and brothers stood outside, wanting to speak to Him. Someone told Him, "Your mother and brothers are standing outside, wanting to speak to You." He replied to him, "Who is My mother, and who are My brothers?" Pointing to His disciples, He said, "Here are My mother and My brothers. For whoever does the will of My Father in heaven is My brother and sister and mother."

Connecting socially with others and getting support from relationships makes perfect sense if your family of origin was a safe place to explore the meaning of close relationships. However, if you were unable to securely attach to your caregivers because their behavior was inconsistent or frightening, it can be terrifying to rely on social relationships to meet our needs. And yet, God still calls us to make Him our Father and to consider fellow believers our family.

Attachment Styles

If you struggle with seeing God as your loving Father or connecting with your church family, you are not alone. If your parents were not loving very often or your social relationships were dangerous, it is natural to have a resistance towards anyone trying to be your caregiver or trying to be your family member. We need supernatural faith to trust God and to trust our brothers and sisters in Christ. Let's take a look at how our attachments with early caregivers affect our relationships and the ability to trust.

The most critical period for attachment happens during the first two years of our lives[32]. Throughout all of our childhood years, development takes place within the context of our attachment to our caregivers[33]. Psychologists have studied different observable patterns that we display when we are around our caregivers as children. These patterns are often called the "attachment style" we had with a caregiver. We can have different attachment behaviors with different caregivers or those who we were in close relationships with as a child[34]. This is because our behavior changed according to how well each caregiver was meeting our needs. The four attachment styles are outlined below.

Secure Attachment

The child uses the caregiver as a secure base for exploration, and the caregiver responds appropriately, promptly, and consistently to the child's needs[35]. According to Dr. Dan Siegel, "Someone with secure attachment…basically says, "I'm worthy of being seen. My emotions are worthwhile[36]." Characteristics of a secure attachment with God are trusting that He has your best interest at heart and He wants to meet your needs. Those with secure attachments believe their needs are valid and express them in relationships.

Avoidant Attachment

With this type of attachment style, the child shows little emotion or affection toward the caregiver, and the caregiver does not respond to the child when he/she is upset[37]. About 20% of the population falls into this category[38]. An avoidant attachment with your caregiver may make you think that the best way to survive is to not need anything from anybody[39]. Dr. Ron Siegel describes it as, "We can go through the world with this avoidance strategy of, I don't really need other people. I'm very independent, and then we wind up feeling hurt when others treat us as though we don't really need other people and we should be able to handle it on our own[40]."

 Characteristics of an avoidant attachment with a caregiver could be difficulty asking God and others for help. Although you want intimacy, you may pull away from it.

Anxious Attachment

With this type of attachment style, the child is ambivalent toward the caregiver, seeking comfort but also pushing the caregiver away. The caregiver responds inconsistently to the child (sometimes attentive and sometimes neglectful[41]). This inconsistency of our caregivers can make us feel anxious, with a need to "rev up" and stay busy[42]. Sometimes our caregiver was too intrusive and close to us and other times they weren't available[43]. Ultimately, this inconsistency can make a child wonder if the caregiver will really be there for her when she needs them[44].

According to Dr. Ron Siegel, "the anxiously attached person...feels, I can't depend on you, and then so quickly picks up on the fault of the other, and then the other gets pushed away because it's like, hey – whatever I do, you seem to tell me I'm not doing it good enough[45]."

Characteristics of an anxious attachment are difficulty relaxing and trusting God and others, and being overly critical of others as a defensive mode. Someone with an anxious attachment may find faults with the very person they want to be close to.

Disorganized Attachment

With this type of attachment style, the child shows contradictory or disoriented behavior, and the caregiver displays frightening, frightened, intrusive, and/or withdrawn behavior toward the child[46]. Contributing factors to disorganized attachment can be domestic violence, maternal depressive disorder or schizophrenia, parental substance abuse, and parental dissociation[47]. When our caregiver was out of reach to us, it placed us in an irresolvable conflict[48]. We had the natural desire to move towards our caregiver and flee danger, yet our own caregiver was the source of our danger[49].

Dr. Alan Sroufe and Dr. Dan Siegel describe this experience as, "This [conflict] activates two brain circuits simultaneously. The attachment circuitry screams out: "Go to my attachment figure for protection!" Yet, at the same time, an even older circuit of survival screams, "Get away from this source of terror!" The same person triggers approach and avoidance, and the infant's capacity for an organized response collapses[50]."

This type of mental conflict destroys our social connections. Dr. Dan Siegel says, "If I have disorganized attachment, I can't regulate my emotions, and I fragment my internal sense of self. Under stress, I cannot think clearly. Mutuality in relationships is really strained, and so I feel like I don't really get much from relationships, so I'd better try to get something from you. It's not a give and take, give and take, like that[51]."

Characteristics of a disorganized attachment are feeling an urge to fight, flee, or freeze around God or others. Anyone attempting to be your caregiver, such as God, may trigger fear. Relationships with others may feel empty.

Repairing Our Attachment with God and Others

Even if you relate with one or more of these attachment styles, the good news is that God did not leave us with our earthly parents. He rescues us and heals us so that we can attach to Him as our caregiver. If our brain develops by forming social connections, then the healthy social connections we make with God and our church family can literally rebuild our brains. The science of epigenetics is just beginning to show what believers have known from the Word of God all along: we can be healed and changed and our future is not fixed. The field of epigenetics examines what makes genes active in one person and go dormant in another person[52]. This area of study shows how our genes can be turned on or off throughout life, based on our environment[53]. Although we have a certain number of genes and DNA that we have inherited from our parents, epigenetics explains how we can actually change and move beyond what we've inherited[54].

We are more than just a collection of genes that were passed down from our parents. We are a spirit that is forever tuned into the Holy Spirit, and we have a soul that is being renewed by God's Word, and we have a body that will be resurrected from the dead when Jesus returns.

Repairing Relationships with Our Children

This ability to change is also good news for those of us who worry we are passing down our trauma to our own children. God created us with a biological need to connect with our parents. Your children's futures are not set in stone. There is still hope for change and restoration because you are now attached to your Father and this will positively affect how you parent your own children. As you experience God's loving rod and staff of discipline, this will change how you discipline your children.

A New Baseline of Safety

It is not too late to form a brand new baseline of safety or to restore a broken baseline of safety because God is now your Father and you are connected with your church family. The following page depicts what a new baseline of safety looks like after trauma.

SPIRIT: *Jesus is my safety net. I am in His arms. He restores all things that happen to me. Psalm 139:5: "You go before me and follow me. You place Your hand of blessing on my head"(NLT). He goes in and repairs my past and goes ahead to my future and already starts planning so that goodness and mercy are waiting for me. Isaiah 61:3: "To all who mourn in Israel, He will give a crown of beauty for ashes"(NLT). When I mourn, He turns my ashes of death into a crown of beauty. Nothing can come into this sacred space between Him and me. I am always safe here. Psalm 27:5: "For He will conceal me there when troubles come; He will hide me in His sanctuary. He will place me out of reach on a high rock"(NLT).*

MIND: *I trust my God-given defense system to know what is safe and what is not. I trust my instincts because God is my leader.*

BODY: *I am a fighter. I will fight to protect myself because I am important. Jesus died for me so that I can live.*

ABOUT THE AUTHOR

Melissa Taylor is a Christian Self-Help author originally from Kennewick, Washington. She has a Bachelor's in Music and a minor in Bible from Southeastern University of the Assemblies of God and a Master of Social Work from Boise State University. After dabbling in ESL teaching and international non-profit work, she began a career as a social worker and non-profit Executive Director. She currently resides in Phoenix, Arizona, with her husband and son.

1 Adapted from Brenda Cochran, LCSW
2 Matt Perman, *What is the Doctrine of the Trinity?* Desiring God. Retrieved from https://www.desiringgod.org/articles/what-is-the-doctrine-of-the-trinity
3 Robert P. Lightner, *The God of the Bible, An Introduction to the Doctrine of God*, Baker Book House, Grand Rapids, 1973, p. 12-13. Retrieved from https://bible.org/seriespage/2-what-god
4 Brenda Cochran, LCSW
5 Bibles for America, *What is the Human Spirit According to the Bible?* Retrieved from https://blog.biblesforamerica.org/what-is-the-human-spirit-in-the-bible/
6 Bibles for America, *What is the Human Spirit According to the Bible?* Retrieved from https://blog.biblesforamerica.org/what-is-the-human-spirit-in-the-bible/
7 Brenda Cochran, LCSW
8 Dr. Ruth Lanius, *Treating Trauma Master Series*, The Neurobiology of Trauma
9 Dr. Ruth Lanius, *Treating Trauma Master Series*, The Neurobiology of Trauma
10 Dr. Dan Siegel, MD. *How to Help Your Client Understand Their Window of Tolerance.* Retrieved from https://www.nicabm.com/trauma-how-to-help-your-clients-understand-their-window-of-tolerance/
11 Brenda Cochran, LCSW
12 Dr. Ron Siegel, Treating Trauma Master Series, The Neurobiology of Attachment
13 *The Body Keeps the Score* by Bessel A. Van der Kolk, Penguin Books
14 *The Body Keeps the Score* by Bessel A. Van der Kolk, Penguin Books
15 Dr. Ruth Ogden, *Treating Trauma Master Series,* The Neurobiology of Attachment
16 Dr. Bessel van der Kolk, *Treating Trauma Master Series,* The Limbic System
17 Dr. Bessel van der Kolk, *Treating Trauma Master Series,* The Limbic System
18 Dr. Bessel van der Kolk, Treating Trauma Master Series, The Limbic System
19 *The Body Keeps the Score* by Bessel A. Van der Kolk, Penguin Books
20 *The Body Keeps the Score* by Bessel A. Van der Kolk, Penguin Books
21 Brenda Cochran, LCSW
22 Child Welfare Trauma Training Toolkit, 1st Edition, January 2013
23 Child Welfare Trauma Training Toolkit, 1st Edition, January 2013
24 Child Welfare Trauma Training Toolkit, 1st Edition, January 2013
25 Child Welfare Trauma Training Toolkit, 1st Edition, January 2013
26 Child Welfare Trauma Training Toolkit, 1st Edition, January 2013
27 Child Welfare Trauma Training Toolkit, 1st Edition, January 2013
28 NCTSN: Caring for Children Who Have Experienced Trauma, 2010
29 NCTSN: Caring for Children Who Have Experienced Trauma, 2010
30 NCTSN: Caring for Children Who Have Experienced Trauma, 2010
31 Reasons for Hope, Jesus, *How are the Shepherd's Rod and Staff different?* Retrieved from https://reasonsforhopejesus.com/shepherds-rod-and-staff-different/

[32] Child Welfare Trauma Training Toolkit, 1st Edition, January 2013
[33] Child Welfare Trauma Training Toolkit, 1st Edition, January 2013
[34] Child Welfare Trauma Training Toolkit, 1st Edition, January 2013
[35] Child Welfare Trauma Training Toolkit, 1st Edition, January 2013
[36] Dr. Dan Siegel, *Treating Trauma Master Series*, The Neurobiology of Attachment
[37] Child Welfare Trauma Training Toolkit, 1st Edition, January 2013
[38] Dr. Dan Siegel, *Treating Trauma Master Series*, The Neurobiology of Attachment
[39] Dr. Dan Siegel, *Treating Trauma Master Series*, The Neurobiology of Attachment
[40] Dr. Ron Siegel, *Treating Trauma Master Series*, The Neurobiology of Attachment
[41] Child Welfare Trauma Training Toolkit, 1st Edition, January 2013
[42] Dr. Dan Siegel, *Treating Trauma Master Series*, The Neurobiology of Attachment
[43] Dr. Dan Siegel, *Treating Trauma Master Series*, The Neurobiology of Attachment
[44] Dr. Dan Siegel, *Treating Trauma Master Series*, The Neurobiology of Attachment
[45] Dr. Ron Siegel, *Treating Trauma Master Series*, The Neurobiology of Attachment
[46] Child Welfare Trauma Training Toolkit, 1st Edition, January 2013
[47] Child Welfare Trauma Training Toolkit, 1st Edition, January 2013
[48] Dr. Alan Sroufe & Dr. Dan Siegel, *The Verdict is In,* Treating Trauma Master Series
[49] Dr. Alan Sroufe & Dr. Dan Siegel, *The Verdict is In,* Treating Trauma Master Series
[50] Dr. Alan Sroufe & Dr. Dan Siegel, *The Verdict is In,* Treating Trauma Master Series
[51] Dr. Dan Siegel, *Treating Trauma Master Series*, The Neurobiology of Attachment
[52] Dr. Ruth Buczynski, *Treating Trauma Master Series*, The Neurobiology of Attachment
[53] Dr. Ruth Buczynski, *Treating Trauma Master Series*, The Neurobiology of Attachment
[54] Dr. Ruth Buczynski, *Treating Trauma Master Series*, The Neurobiology of Attachment

Made in United States
Troutdale, OR
02/19/2025

29107354R00036